STUMBLING GIANTS

Transforming Canada's Banks for the Information Age